The Laming Family of Kent England

by Lorine McGinnis Schulze

ISBN: 978-1-987938-14-2
Publisher Olive Tree Genealogy

Over the last 40 plus years I have researched and gathered a great deal of information and uncovered many documents for my mother's ancestors in England. Pondering how best to preserve my research and share the stories of these maternal ancestors, I decided to compile books on each family surname.

Because the books were written for family, I have not cited my sources nor have I written long chapters of anecdotal stories. Instead I opted to create a chronological timeline for each generation. Images for all baptismal, marriage, burial, land records and so on that were discovered for each ancestor are also included.

If siblings were found, family group sheets are included. If they were not found, only my direct ancestor is noted. At the end of the book you will find blank pages for your own notes.

Those who want to know my sources can contact me directly through my website Olive Tree Genealogy at www.OliveTreeGenealogy.com My email is found at the bottom of each page.

I hope that readers enjoy these books and the stories of the ancestors.

Lorine McGinnis Schulze

Table of Contents

Researching the Laming Family

The Laming family has been challenging to research. First there is the problem of early needed church records not surviving. Secondly the surname is quite common in the Thanet area of Kent which is where the family lived for many generations.

Add to that many Laming individuals of the same approximate age bearing the same first name! For example in this 6-generation book, the direct line from William Laming born circa 1610 to Henry Laming born in 1791 has three ancestors named William and two named John. So family groups might consist of a man named William with a cousin named John, both naming sons born in the same years John and William.

The most challenging item to find for this family were their burial records. Burial records from the 17th and 18th centuries in Kent do not normally provide ages of the deceased, or any information other than their name and burial date. Look for the burial of a man named William Laming with the only clue to his death the fact that his last known child was born in a certain year, and that he baptised all his children in one specific church, you will still find dozens of William Laming burials in that church in time periods that could be him.

In spite of the difficulties I have gathered as much information as I could and hope that descendants will find it useful and interesting.

Generation 1: William Laming ca 1610-? & Mary Cullmer

My 9th great-grandfather William Laming and Mary Cullmer (aka Colmer) were married 23 October 1645 in Saint Laurence, Thanet, Kent

St. Lawrence Church, Ramsgate.

Mary's baptism took place in St. Peter in Thanet 17 March 1617 to John Cullmer and Margaret Samson. William's baptismal record has not been found so we cannot provide parents' names for him.

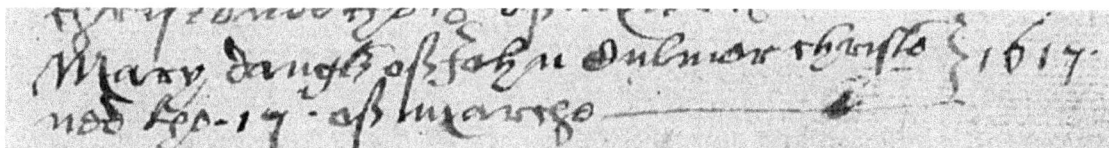

Baptism Mary Culmer 1617. Mary daughter of John Culmer and Margaret, was baptised 17 of March. 1617

St. Peter's Church. (Isle of Thanet.)

The marriage of Mary's parents was found in the church registers for St. Peter, Thanet in 1600

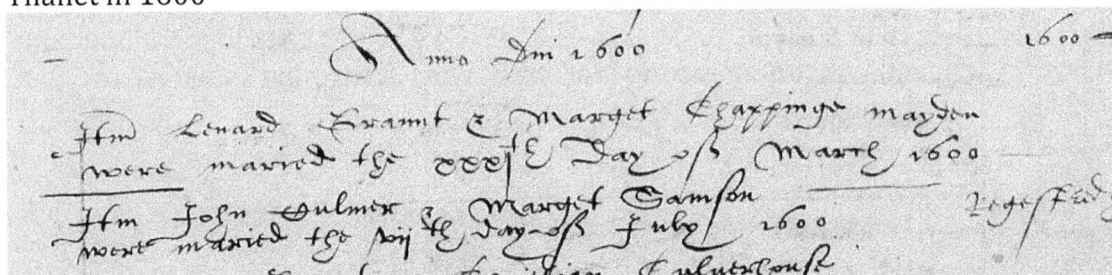

Bottom entry: John Culmer & Margaret Samson were married 7 July 1600

Family Group Sheet for William Laming

Husband:		William Laming
	b:	Bef. 1625
	m:	23 Oct 1645 in Saint Laurence, Thanet, Kent, Eng
	Father:	
	Mother:	
Wife:		Mary Cullmer
	b:	17 Mar 1616/17 in St. Peter, Thanet, Kent, Eng
	Father:	John Cullmer
	Mother:	Margaret Samson
Children:		
1	Name:	Mary Laming
F	b:	08 Feb 1647/48 in St. Lawrence, Thanet, Kent, Eng
2	Name:	Elizabeth Laming
F	b:	31 Aug 1651 in St Peter in Thanet, St Peter
3	Name:	Peter Laming
M	b:	22 Jun 1655 in St Lawrence in Thanet, St Lawrence
4	Name:	William Laming
M	b:	25 Nov 1660 in St. Peter, Thanet, Kent, Eng
	m:	14 Oct 1684 in St. Mary, Minster, Kent Eng.
	Spouse:	Elizabeth Sanders

Notes:

Generation 2: William Laming 1660-? & Elizabeth Sanders

My 8th great-grandfather William Laming was baptised 25 November 1660 in St. Peter in Thanet Kent. William and Elizabeth Sanders were married 14 October 1684 in St. Mary, Minster, Kent

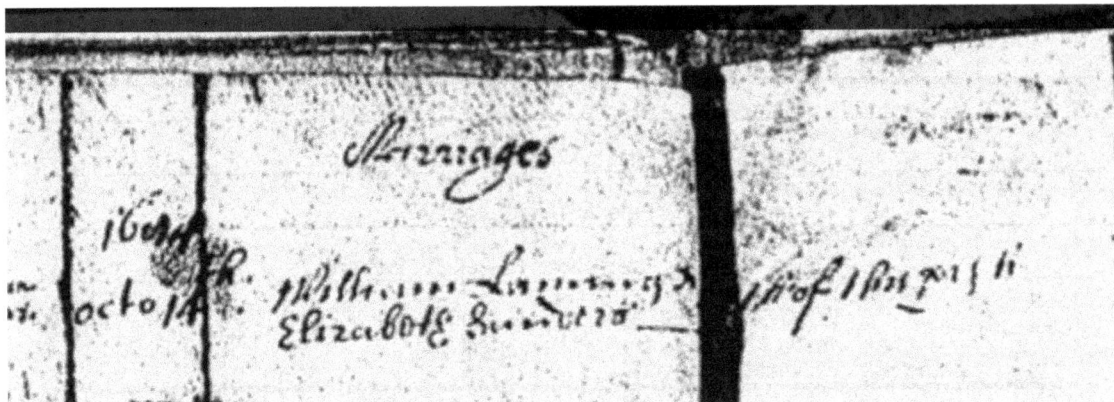

Marriage 1684 William Landing & Elizabeth Sanders

St. Mary's Church   Reading

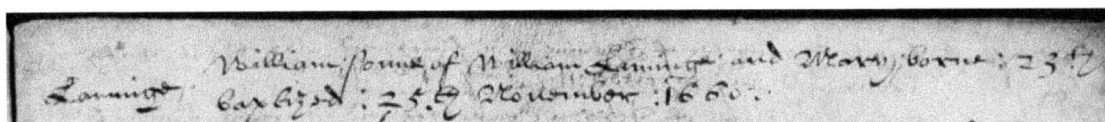

Baptism William 25 November 1660 in St. Peter in Thanet

Family Group Sheet for William Laming

Husband:		William Laming
	b:	25 Nov 1660 in St. Peter, Thanet, Kent, Eng
	m:	14 Oct 1684 in St. Mary, Minster, Kent Eng.
	Father:	William Laming
	Mother:	Mary Cullmer
Wife:		Elizabeth Sanders
	Father:	
	Mother:	
Children:		
1	Name:	John Laming
M	b:	02 Aug 1685 in St. Mary, Minster, Kent Eng.
	m:	05 Jan 1713/14 in St. Mary, Minster, Kent Eng.
	Spouse:	Mary Stephens
2	Name:	William Laming
M	b:	11 Sep 1687
3	Name:	Elizabeth Laming
F	b:	16 Feb 1689/90
4	Name:	Mary Laming
F	b:	17 Feb 1691/92

Generation 3: John Laming 1685-? & Mary Stephens

My 7th great-grandfather John Laming was baptised 02 August 1685 in St. Mary Minster. John and Mary Stephens were married 05 January 1713 in St. Mary the Virgin, Minster, Kent

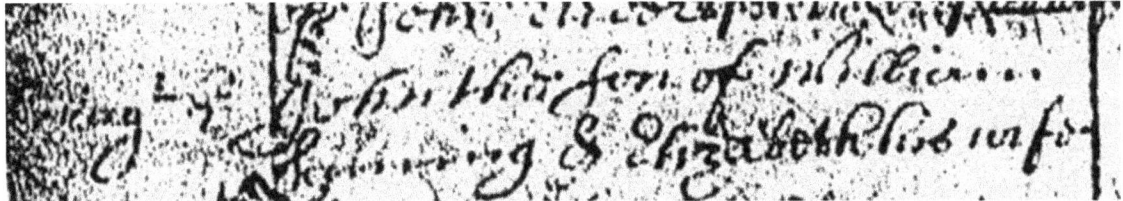

Baptism John Laming son of William and Elizabeth. 1685

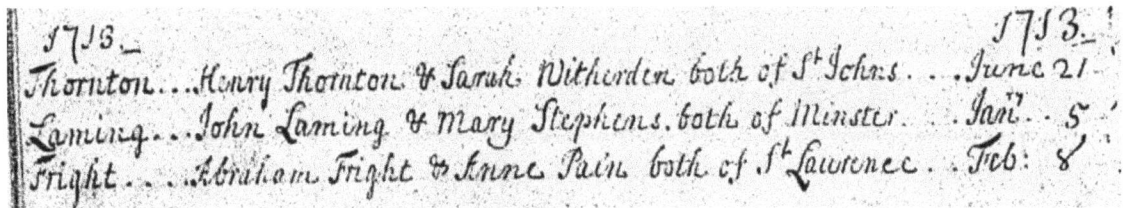

Marriage Laming – Stephens both of Minster. 1713

Mary Stephens was baptised 24 May 1690 in St. Mary, Minster Thanet to parents Peter Stevens (sic) and Elizabeth (nee Creest re marriage to Peter, but Kris? at baptism of daughter Mary)

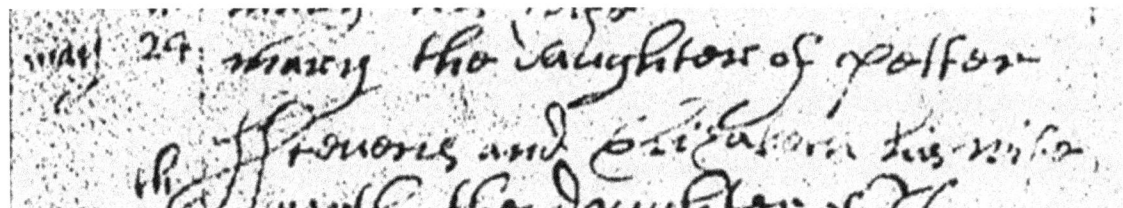

Baptism Mary daughter of Peter & Elizabeth Stevens 1690

Family Group Sheet for John Laming

Husband:		John Laming
	b:	02 Aug 1685 in St. Mary, Minster, Kent Eng.
	m:	05 Jan 1713/14 in St. Mary, Minster, Kent Eng.
	Father:	William Laming
	Mother:	Elizabeth Sanders
Wife:		Mary Stephens
	b:	24 May 1690 in St. Marys, Minster in Thanet, Kent
	Father:	Peter Stephens
	Mother:	Elizabeth Creest
Children:		
1	Name:	Elizabeth Laming
F	b:	12 Dec 1714 in St. Mary, Minster, Kent
2	Name:	John Laming
M	b:	15 Apr 1716 in St. Mary, Minster, Kent Eng.
	m:	26 Nov 1748 in Cathedral, Canterbury, Kent Eng
	Spouse:	Mary Noldred
3	Name:	Peter Laming
M	b:	09 Jun 1717 in St. Marys, Minster Kent

Generation 4: John Laming 1716-? & Mary Noldred

My 6th great-grandfather John Laming was baptised 15 April 1716 in St. Mary Minster. He married Mary Noldred in Canterbury Cathedral on 26 November 1748

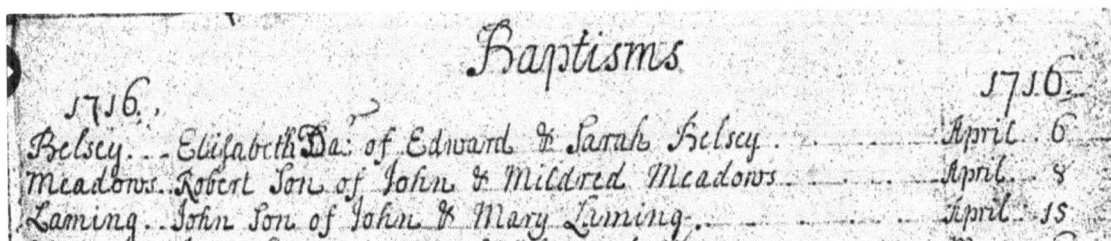

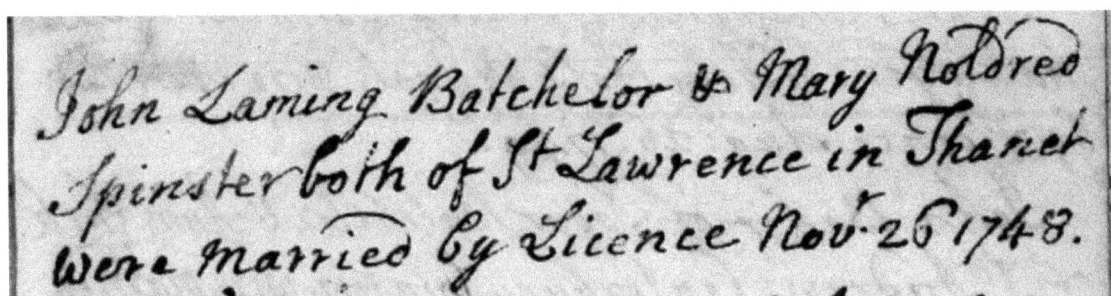

Marriage 1648 John Laming & Mary Noldred

Mary was baptised 28 May 1721 in St. Lawrence, Thanet, Kent to parents Henry Noldred and Mary Goodson.

Family Group Sheet for John Laming

Husband:		John Laming
	b:	15 Apr 1716 in St. Mary, Minster, Kent Eng.
	m:	26 Nov 1748 in Cathedral, Canterbury, Kent Eng
	Father:	John Laming
	Mother:	Mary Stephens
Wife:		Mary Noldred
	b:	28 May 1721 in St. Lawrence, Thanet, Kent Eng.
	Father:	Henry Noldred
	Mother:	Mary Goodson
Children:		
1	Name:	John Laming
M	b:	28 Jul 1751
2	Name:	Mary Laming
F	b:	18 Nov 1753
3	Name:	William Laming
M	b:	30 Oct 1757 in St. Lawrence, Thanet, Kent Eng.
	m:	08 Oct 1786 in St. Laurence, Thanet, Kent Eng.
	Spouse:	Jane Hooper

Generation 5: William Laming 1757-? & Jane Hooper

My 5th great-grandfather William Laming was baptised 30 Oct 1757 in St. Laurence, Thanet.

Baptism of William Laming 1757

Kentish Gazette - Wednesday 03 February 1779

William and the widow Jane Philpot (nee Jane Hooper) married on 08 October 1786 in St. Laurence, Thanet Kent

Jane Hooper was baptised on 27 May 1728 at St. Laurence in Thanet to Stephen Hooper and Ann Herbert.

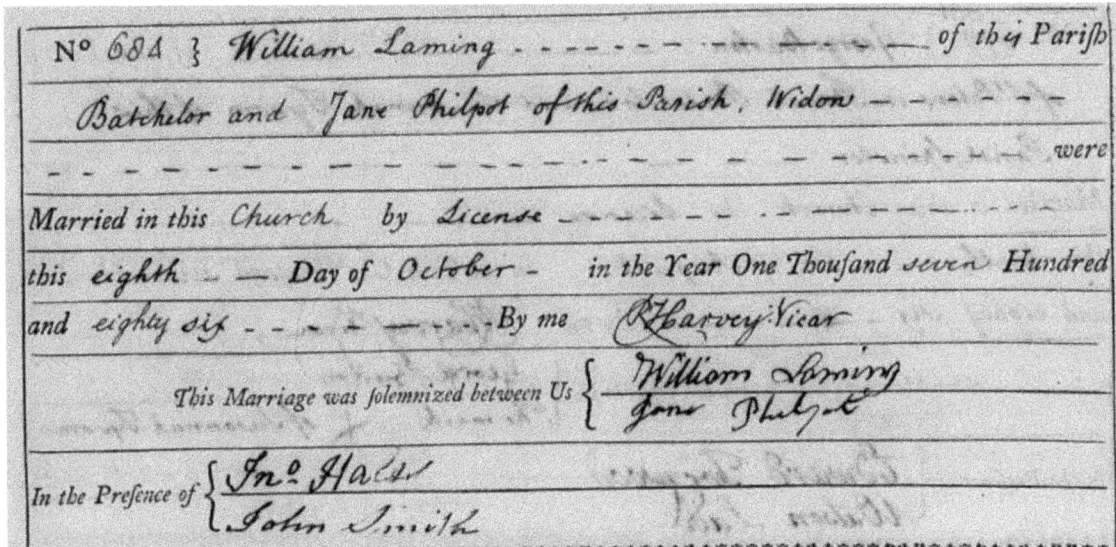

Jane was previously married to Thomas Philpott. Their marriage took place on 02 April 1782 in St. Laurence, Thanet, Kent. Poor Jane's marriage was short-lived as Thomas was buried in St. Laurence two years later.

A male child named Edward was baptised 22 Apr 1784 at Hackington, St Stephen to a Thomas and Jane Philpot and it is very possible this is Jane Hooper.

Om 1808, when Jane's youngest son was only five years old, she died of "decline" and was buried in the church cemetery at St. Laurence in Thanet.

Jane Laming Burial 1808

Family Group Sheet for William Laming

Husband:		William Laming
	b:	30 Oct 1757 in St. Lawrence, Thanet, Kent Eng.
	m:	08 Oct 1786 in St. Laurence, Thanet, Kent Eng.
	Father:	John Laming
	Mother:	Mary Noldred
Wife:		Jane Hooper
	b:	06 Aug 1760 in St. Laurence, Thanet, Kent Eng.
	d:	15 Nov 1808 in St. Laurence, Thanet, Kent England
	Father:	Stephen Hooper
	Mother:	Ann Herbert
Children:		
1	Name:	John Hooper Laming
M	b:	21 Jan 1787
2	Name:	William Laming
M	b:	17 Aug 1788
3	Name:	Henry Laming
M	b:	06 Apr 1791 in St. Lawrence, Thanet, Kent Eng.
	m:	13 Jul 1814 in St. Laurence, Thanet, Kent Eng.
	Spouse:	Mary Smith
4	Name:	Samuel Noldred Laming
M	b:	17 Nov 1793
5	Name:	Jane Hooper Laming
F	b:	13 Nov 1796
6	Name:	Mary Ann Laming
F	b:	21 Dec 1800
7	Name:	Stephen Hooper Laming
M	b:	10 Jul 1803

Generation 6: Henry Laming 1791-? & Mary Smith

My 4th great-grandfather Henry Laming was born March 7 and baptised April 6, 1791 to William and Jane Laming.

Henry married Mary Smith in St. Laurence in Thanet on 13 July 1814. She was born May 17 and baptised 25 May 1783 in t. Laurence, Thanet to William Smith and Catherine Panterey.

Tuesday 22 October 1833, Kentish Weekly Post or Canterbury Journal, Kent, England 2 Articles

City of Canterbury Sessions.

These Sessions commenced on Thursday last, in the Guildhall, before Richard Frend esq, Mayor, the Chamberlain, Recorder, and a bench of Magistrates. There were no cases of parish appeal before the Court.

The grand Jury having been sworn, the names of several persons bound over to keep the peace were called, and the parties discharged on making their appearance, and paying the customary fee.

The Recorder addressed the Grand Jury. He observed he was happy in having it in his power to say that there were few cases before them, requiring their consideration, and those were not of a serious magnitude. There were only two cases of common larceny; and one of felony, whereby the parties, who were charged in the indictment, were on bail. The name of one of the women was Mary Brown, and the other Mary Ann ___. They were indicted for stealing a watch, the property of a person named Henry Laming. It would be for the Jury to say whether these two women were both concerned in the robbery, or whether the act was committed by one of them. This was a point which would require some nicety, and, if, after mature deliberation they should agree that both women were implicated they would return a true bill; on the contrary, if one of them should appear to be involved in the commission of the offence, they would of course give the other prisoner the benefit of any doubt which might arise, and, of course return a true bill against one of them. If they thought the watch was lost without the interference of the prisoners, then it would be necessary to dismiss the case altogether. It would be recollected that the affair took place under circumstances which did not reflect much credit upon the prosecutor; notwithstanding if it should seem that a felony had been committed, – if it should appear that he had been robbed by the parties indicted, the Jury would of course return them for trial.

ST. MARY, DOVER, APPELLANT. ST. MARY MAGDALEN, RESPONDENTS.

Mr. Grevener, of Dover, of the firm of Grevener and Shrewsbury, applied to the Court to enter a respite in the above case.

The Recorder said counsel were not present, and perhaps it would be better to await their arrival.

Mr. Grevener observed, that he was willing to give them the advantage of the fee.—His request to enter a respite arose from a desire to despatch.

An hour having passed, Mr. Grevener renewed his application. The Town Clerk observed, Counsel had been sent for, and, most probably would be present in a short time.

Mr. Grevener bowed, and again resumed his seat.

A few minutes elapsed, when a letter was handed to Mr. Nutt. It was from the Counsel, who, it appearing having ascertained that there were no cases requiring legal ingenuity, intimated their intention absenting themselves.

Mr. Grevener.—I presume, Sir, I may now renew my application, since the gentlemen of the bar, have notified to the Court, that they do not intend to be present.

Town Clerk.—Perhaps we had better send for one of them.

Mr. Grevener.—No.—I shall avail myself of the absence, in order that the parish I represent, may enjoy the advantage of it.—I am not to throw a fee in when the business can be transacted without them.

The respite was then entered.

Stephen Else appeared at the bar, to answer to

My Laming line died out when Henry and Mary's daughter Mary Laming, my 3rd great-grandmother, was born in 1818 in Thanet Kent. She married John Henry Caspall and that is another book.

Notes

www.ingramcontent.com/pod-product-compliance
Lightning Source LLC
Chambersburg PA
CBHW051350290326
41933CB00042B/3356